AF089120

Nicholas Garland

I wish ...

Published in 2007 by

THE WAYWISER PRESS

9 Woodstock Road, London N4 3ET, UK
P.O. Box 6205, Baltimore, MD 21206, USA

www.waywiser-press.com

Copyright © Nicholas Garland, 2007

The right of Nicholas Garland to be identified as the author of this work has been
asserted by him in accordance with the Copyright, Designs and Patents Act of 1988.

All rights reserved.

A CIP catalogue record for this book is available from the British Library.

Numbers 1-150, signed
ISBN-10: 1-904130-24-0; ISBN-13: 978-1-904130-24-6

Numbers 151-400, unsigned
ISBN-10: 1-904130-25-9; ISBN-13: 978-1-904130-25-3

Printed and bound by
BAS Printers, Romsey, Hampshire

for Esme

Contents

I wish I were a Gorillaranimus

I wish I were a Crococodilicus

I wish I were a Tough Armadillio

I wish I were an Octoctopusaurus

I wish I were a Leo Majesticus

I wish I were a Pythonapullerus

I wish I were a White Albatrossius

I wish I were a Hyena Humorous

I wish I were a Hippopopotamus

I wish I were a Bad-Tempered Camelus

I wish I were an Elephantiaphus

Contents

I wish I were a Sleek Dolphinarial

I wish I were a Ferocious Tigeris

I wish I were an Ursus Horribilis

I wish I were a Rhinoscereeacus

I wish I were a Lupus Lunaticus

I wish I were a Gentle Giraffaloft

I wish I were a Levileviathan

A Note about Nicholas Garland

Acknowledgements

Colophon

I wish I were a Gorillaranimus

And could beat a stunning rhythm on my chest.

But oh! I am not,

Alas! I cannot be

A Gorillari-Gorillaranimus.

But I'm a skeeter,

A quick will o' the wisp,

I can vanish in the blinking of an eye.

I wish I were a Crococodilicus,

Like a U-Boat armed with rows and rows of teeth.

But oh! I am not,

Alas! I cannot be

A Crocodillo-Crococodilicus.

But I'm a mayfly,

A gone-tomorrow pal,

I celebrate my birthday all my life.

I wish I were a Tough Armadillio

Like an armoured tank protected every side.

But oh! I am not,

Alas! I cannot be

Completely shielded – quite safe from any harm.

But I'm a spider,

A dusky scuttle quick,

And I float like Tarzan swinging on a vine.

I wish I were an Octoctopusaurus

And could rocket by in clouds of Indian Ink.

But oh! I am not,

Alas! I cannot be

An Octoporous-Octoctopusaurus.

But I'm a drone-bee,

A buzzing work-a-day,

And I airlift food all summer for my Queen.

I wish I were a Leo Majesticus,

Fit to decorate a monarch's coat of arms.

But oh! I am not,

Alas! I cannot be

Nature's paragon, a fearless superstar.

But I'm a worker,

An ant who slaves all day,

Shifting burdens that are fifty times my weight.

I wish I were a Pythonapullerus

With coils to make a buffalo short of breath.

But oh! I am not,

Alas! I cannot be

A Pythonori-Pythonapullerus.

But I'm a flit-past

And I'm a butterfly,

I can pause and make myself look like a leaf.

I wish I were a White Albatrossacross,

Gliding, effortless, above the wide, wide sea.

But oh! I am not,

Alas! I cannot be

A sailor's escort towards the setting sun.

But I'm a Sea Horse,

A bucking bronco fish,

I can ride the briny range beneath the waves.

I wish I were a Hyena Humorous,

Sure to greet success and failure with a grin.

But oh! I am not,

Alas! I cannot be

A smiling hunter, hyena chuckle-head.

But I'm a House Fly,

Musca Domesticus,

I can walk on any surface upside-down.

I wish I were a Hippopopotamus

And could gallop under water very fast.

But oh! I am not,

Alas! I cannot be

A Hippopopo-Hippopopotamus.

But I'm a tadpole,

A tiny wriggle-job,

And when I grow up I'm gonna be a frog.

I wish I were a Bad-Tempered Camelus

And could live on thorns for days without a drink.

But oh! I am not,

Alas! I cannot be

A cool survivor in trackless desert sand.

But I'm a Grasshop

And I'm a Katydid,

I can play the fiddle with my left hind-leg.

I wish I were an Elephantiaphus

And could pick off the coconuts with my nose.

But oh! I am not,

Alas! I cannot be

An Elephanti-Elephantiaphus.

But I'm a cockroach

And I'm a water-bug,

I can crawl around and hide behind the sink.

I wish I were a Sleek Dolphinarial

With the open sea my playground and my home.

But oh! I am not,

Alas! I cannot be

A non-stop show-off, an ocean acrobat.

But I'm a Sprat-Fish,

Too small to notice much,

Just a flash of silver light and I am gone.

I wish I were a Ferocious Tigeris

And could scare the jungle with my golden eyes.

But oh! I am not,

Alas! I cannot be

A prowling hunter – a scowling Tigercat.

But I'm a lowlife

And I'm a centipede,

I am speedy on account of all my legs.

I wish I were an Ursus Horribilis,

A colossus made of muscle, teeth and claws.

But oh! I am not,

Alas! I cannot be

A forest bruiser who doesn't give a damn.

But I'm a Flea-skite,

Yeah, I'm a long-jump champ,

And when trouble comes, with one bound I am free.

I wish I were a Rhinoscereeacus

And could wear an ivory toothpick on my nose.

But oh! I am not,

Alas! I cannot be

A Rhinoscori-Rhinoscereeacus.

But I'm a firefly,

And I'm a lightning bug,

I can start a conflagration with my tail.

I wish I were a Lupus Lunaticus,

Chasing down the deer and howling at the moon.

But oh! I am not,

Alas! I cannot be

A fierce grey hunter, the leader of the pack.

But I'm a beetle

And I'm a pumpkin-bug,

I can buzz and bang my head against the wall.

I wish I were a Gentle Giraffaloft

And could reach the branches others cannot see.

But oh! I am not,

Alas! I cannot be

The tallest grazer, a strolling minaret.

But I'm a Lady,

A scarlet brooch on legs,

I adorn the leaves and twigs on which I stand.

I wish I were a Levileviathan,

Spouting, singing, swimming slowly 'cross the sea.

But oh! I am not,

Alas! I cannot be

A moving island, an awesome mass of Whale.

But I'm a limpet,

A piece of living rock,

I can cling to one reef till the end of time.

A Note about Nicholas Garland

Nicholas Garland was born in London in 1935. He moved with his family to New Zealand in 1947 and lived there until 1954, when he returned to London to attend the Slade School of Art.

For some years he worked as a stage manager and theatre director. Then, in 1966, he joined the *Daily Telegraph* as their first political cartoonist. He moved to *The Independent* in 1984, but in 1991 rejoined the *Telegraph*, where he remains to this day.

As well as being a cartoonist, Garland is an accomplished painter and woodcut artist, whose work has been exhibited widely. He has also illustrated a number of books, most recently *The Coma*, by his son Alex Garland.

Acknowledgements

Some of the verses included in this book are adapted from an anonymously authored sequence which W. H. Auden and John Garrett included in their 1952 anthology, *The Poet's Tongue*. The other verses included here were written by Nicholas Garland.

I wish ...

is set in Adobe Garamond type and printed on 170 gsm Satimat club paper.

There are 400 numbered copies, of which the first 150 are signed.

The book was designed and typeset by Philip Hoy at

THE WAYWISER PRESS

This is copy
349